FLESH AND FLOWERS

For P.J.B.R.

ANNE LEWIS-SMITH

Flesh
and
Flowers

Mitre Press · London

52 LINCOLN'S INN FIELDS, W.C.2.

Acknowledgment is made to the
following magazines and anthologies in
which some of these poems first appeared

Envoi, Scrip, Breakthru', Limbo (Canada),
*Manifold, Poetmeat, Extra Verse,
Chase, Origins and Diversions, Outposts,
The Poet* (India), *We Offer—,
Expression, The Scillonian, Target,
Spring Anthology 1965, 1966, 1967, Love Poems* (Ken Geering)
and *Victims of Our Fear* (Poetmeat)

*Printed in Gt. Britain for
The Mitre Press (Fudge & Co. Ltd.)*

Contents

Contents (cont.)

FLESH

RETURN

I went back.

After four years I went back,
and the grassy track
was foot marked mud,
our bracken bed
pock marked mud.

Oh God, did my head
lie there?

—and the firs?
the whispering witnesses?
felled and branch bare,
leaving the sky
empty.

Was this the reason why
I promised
not to go back?

YESTERDAY

Wanting you—
    your arms—
        your mouth—
           you—
I stood in the cellar
talking of wine
and listening to the
noise of dancing
and you politely
answering.
Then no words
for a crystal moment,
only the eyes asking
before we moved
together.
Now I want you
    your arms
        your mouth
           you—

RICHARD

This time tomorrow you will be going
luggage in hand down the narrow stone quay,
Fishermen say this wind will be blowing
west, when you go on the tumbled grey sea.
This time tomorrow you will be leaving
waving your hand as you clamber aboard
telling us there, and we half believing,
that you will be back, our friendships restored.
We shall be standing and watching your boat
dip in the waves as she takes you away,
straining our eyes as the brown of your coat
blurs in the distance to uniform grey.

—and I—I shall say as I turn away
the tears on my face are only salt spray.

CARN NEAR—ISLES OF SCILLY

Is anyone there but you?
Does the early haze still cling
to St Agnes, and has the dew
left pin point tears on the ling?
Have the birds stopped screaming now you are still,
can you hear the water slap each stone
and rabbits rustle the heathery hill?
Are you alone?

Now quickly before they come, carrying lunch and tea,
climb the westerly rocks, high huddled over the sea,
and tell me, tell me
can you see
hidden on Samson
our tamarisk tree?

BRACKEN

Love me now, my love,
on last year's tarnished bracken bed
so I can watch above your head
the fresh green tongues curl
on their rigid stems.

Love me now, my love,
while the prying pink foxglove
looks down each tunnelled eye
to where we hidden lie.
Where you and I
can watch the spider spin
her narrow rope
across our secret sky.

2nd CLASS SLEEPER

Love me again,
let the dry blind
rattle on the rain
hit pane.
Your empty coat
swings out into the air
clings flat onto the wall
swings out—
and all
the time, cramped
in this coffined bunk
our bodies race
the train.
Love me again
again, again,
    again—

LLYN CWM BYCHAN

Lying beside you
under the midge-mildewed sky,
with the dark stoned mountains
slipping into the lake,
I knew the cuckoo
and the small wave slap
would echo only in my mind,
and the rough turf on my legs
soon be forgotten harshness.
—and you my love
will you remember this?
Will you remember me?

PRELUDE

Writing our names
yours and mine
on the misted glass,
the finger lines
become clear—
clouds passing
zebra in the letters.

Suddenly each curve
drags with water
then runs swerving
transparently down
making our names long leg'd
nonsensical, drowning
the blur in clarity.

I sponged the window clean
then mopped our watered names.

Remember now——
you found me leaning
when you came
by one wiped window
and one misted pane?

HANDS

Why are my hands
not different?
Why when my eyes
are candles with your loving
should these hands
stay so plain?
When I remember
how our mouths' warmth
melted to each other,
my whole face flowers.
Yet when I recollect
the long length of your back
move underneath
my happy hands,
my fingers
on your thigh—
remembering all your nakedness—
I do not understand
how these two hands
could stay unchanged.

17

ORION

I stood in the night
waiting,
waiting to feel
your hands upon
my shoulders
and your voice say
"that's Orion".

Waited
for your shielding warmth,
your mouth on
my night cooled eyes
for your head
to blot out the skies.

I stood in the night
alone,
and no doubt,
somewhere,
Orion shone
on you.

SPRING?

I do not think that Spring
comes with lambs, daffodils,
crocus, anything
like that.
No ordered season,
but this sudden
wakening
to find each dawning day
unpetaled to your sun.

—so when you go
will it be winter snow,
bitter rain?
Will all this flowering
die again?

PAST MIDNIGHT

When you went,
day, who had pushed her nearness
in our thoughts,
stepped back to her proper place
so the night was long again.
The wind sent
a bare rose branch knocking
knocking at the window,
while black rain
wept
and I—after a lifetime
curled in my memories—
slept.

IS THIS THE WAY TO ... ?

Is this the way to forget?
the unknown mouth wet
the stranger hands
the "why not"
in my ear.
To be an ocean
for unchartered boats
yet never crest a wave.
Gin numbs the flesh
for strange tongues seeking
and substitutes your arms for—
        For what—?
An hour?
a half dream
lost when waking?
Clinging to the night
I fight
each day alone.

HALFWAY

Waiting
halfway down the stairs,
I watched you
in the mirror
come to me.
Saw in the glass
your hands pass
either side of me
before they touched
my back
to draw me close.

—and I was in your arms
halfway down the stairs.
Or was it
halfway up—?

BRANCASTER

I walked the beach alone today
no one was there—
a single track of sand-dents
trailed behind me,
and I smiled
at the faded feel of your hand.

Later,
deep in the dunes,
the sand ran hour-glass
through my fingers
as I sifted thoughts of you,
then lay content
in the well loved bowl
of years ago.

It was only coming back
glad with memories
that I remembered
how I wept.

FUSION

Mouthless I am, my lips dissolved by yours
in this long gentleness.
Your hands pass through me
as I swim into your flesh.
Only your eye, my eye, watches, closes,
then spins away.

Suddenly the hard intrusion of your tongue
sharpens my outline,
leaves your fingers outside
and my mouth its own again.
Then a moment, a breath alone before
I melt in you.

—and I am gone, I heard me sigh
but saw myself no more.

LINNETS AT DINGLI CLIFFS

There are linnets in the small stone house
whose balcony puts out cold wings
over the high cliffs.
Linnets and goldfinch in ten-inch cages,
and the man who caught them brings
seeds and water,
—but not freedom.
Eight hundred feet below the sea is slow,
cliff shadows shrivel in the light
small birds fly high.
Here, slipping between wood bars, cool teasing winds
remind the linnets of their last free flight
but cannot lift their wings.

THE LAST MEETING

I shall not turn my head again
nor bare my eyes to you,
I shall not touch your hand again
nor lift my lips to you,
—but Oh my love, again, again
my heart will ache for you.

OCTOBER LOVE

Was nothing there? No resin smelling pine,
no mushrooms, moss, or fingers touching mine,
no empty cottage, no-one there to play
the broken old piano in the shed?
—and did I dream I turned to walk away
but hands caressed me, lips on my lips said
no-one was watching, why then should I go?
Was I alone when suddenly I found
the soft mimosa gold where none should grow,
and was there no-one wrapped their arms around
me crying "celebrate"? Was there no kiss?
Ah love, there is no word of truth in this.
It was all there, kisses, mimosa tree,
but things as these are not for all to see.

RAIN IN VALETTA

Watching you walk away
across rainshone marble
your feet, for an instant,
made clear marks
till the wet covered them
with a sky mirror.

I remember Saturday
when you came
bringing inside dark prints
on the dry floor,
they faded fast.

Will there always be
no reminder of your coming
or your going——?

MILESTONE

Now you are gone
all ache
all yearning
gone.
This—the last place
where memories cling
has emptied
of remembering
and I am free.
Free of your voice,
the echo of your laugh—
all memory
has gone.

Oh pity me
my love
who cannot now
remember you.

WASTE NOT THESE HOURS

Quick—kiss me again,
time and my youth are slipping,
waste not these hours
in talk my love, come lipping.

WISHFUL THINKING

Perhaps I would rather you did not come
    and then
I should always be waiting,
    and you
would always be coming
    to me.
There would be no farewell
    because
you had not come, no welcome
    for you
would then have never gone.

We were talking
about you—
your name
clearly
on other people's
lips.
I prefer
your name
when I say it—
softly
against
your mouth.

WRISTWATCH

Your watch
lying beside my ear
is loud as Big Ben.
Ticking
illicit minutes
out of step
with your pulse
it has jerked seconds
against my skin
whilst you slept.
Soon I will
turn my head
to see its face
then nudge you
from your dreams
that you might go.
Soon I will
turn my head
—but oh my love
not yet—
time ticks too fast,
in half an hour
this will be past.

33

c

TERZA RIMA

This is a mistake, I know it
but do not by the hesitation
in your dark eyes smiling show it.

This is wrong this visitation
to turn a summer moment's knowing
to the bond of love's relation.

I should not come, but the swift flowing
of my eager pen's-tongue brought me :
since I am, let not my going

be with sadness. Say you sought me
seek me still, so no deflation
drains the joy of what you taught me.

5 A.M.

Light, the Surgeon's knife
has made a neat incision
in the dark
that filled this room,
and day has probed the wound
to show it bare.
Bare to the eye—
but standing here
I feel again your mouth
ignore these lips
to slip the warm length
of my neck,
when all the dawns of time
at that flamed touch,
broke in a trembling
bright extravagance.

THOUGHTS ALONE

How shall I remember you?
Will my eyes
watching each day go
fade out your face?
My hands writing this
forget the feel of yours?
My lips through talking
dim your kiss?
—and will my body
after this
forget the song of yours?

Sometimes I know
this will be true,
a day will pass
without a thought of you.
But equally as true
I know that memories
will flood me through and through
and I will feel
your arms again.

LOVE LETTER

I tear your letter now,
across, across,
and its brief blossom
written years ago
drifts to my earthheld feet
like petalled snow.

Full well I know, I knew
each word, each word
your loving longing
on each page spoke true.
What use your letters now
when I have you?

BLUE TUESDAY

There is no use
in listening
these ears
are wearied,
my eyes abuse
each sunrise
with their tears,
and my lips
have no smile
on them.
So long awhile
my love
since you were here
and I alive.

AFTER SUPPER

I am tired—
I feel your lips
upon my neck
but that is all—
I have no wish
even to lean my cheek
against your hair.
My hands
(in reflex) copy yours
but my mind
is on wallpaper.
Our dry mouths move
together separately
hard as our bodies.
I am tired,
or are you
tired of me?

DRINKS AT 7

An hour ago
I sat polite,
whisky tumblered
but polite—
Do you know
so and so?
and slowly
slowly
getting tight.

Now in my Hotel room
I sober up
on coffee
and alone.
The empty cup
the loud watch
and the voiceless
telephone.

DANGER LANTERN

I thought how warm
the red light looked
across the road—
but when I put
my hand into
the glow,
my fingers were
stained glass
and cold.

FLOWERS

THE GOD-DAUGHTER

Hers was the lamb shy early spring
the gentle bud half opening
but now unpetalled.
    The primrose smile, the fairy ring
    of laughter light about her lips.

Hers was the youth of little things
warm trust in all small feathered wings
but now enfolded.
    Wide eyed as loving hands made strings
    of daisies for her soft hairs crown.

Hers was springtime magic, bringing
music with pale harebells ringing
now an elegy.
    Hers the endless summer singing
    ours the winter of her going.

HOLKHAM

Now having talked to you
    I remember the quiet—
remember pink petalled shells
wind bowled on the beach
tinkling tiny bells,
the white sand low-tide-island
with still hollows, and
the tall pines a high fence
for the flat fen land.
    I remember the quiet—
watching a hare lollop
over dry pine needles,
never seeing me,
and the gentle free
sea laden breeze
combing the maram.
    I remember the quiet—
perhaps when you
walk under the pines,
and the wind breathes through
the high sighing branches,
you will remember me
telling you this
and live my memory.

BASEMENT

Rain is jumping by me on the steps down.
Level with my eyes the road splashes
and then is sky, as the wet wall rises.
The cold key sticks, clicks
and stale smoke welcomes
with the drumming rain outside.

Quick light the match, cap up
peel back the sleeve
before the ceiling shadows drip
black down to drown us.
Band the flesh until
the blue snake shows.

Rain is a funeral drum.

Now the sharpness
Hit,
Hit first, hit true
and watch the thread
of thin blood running back
to mix—
Kick
Kick
Kick

What jazz
there is in rain
the hot drums
dancing,
let us lie
and dance.

LONDON FROM GREENWICH HILL

Reverse the stars!
Fling down the curdled milky way
and band the sleeping Thames
with moonbeams on its dreaming throat.
Here from this night wide attic'd eye
I see the heavens bare,
for all the starry firmament
lies at my feet.

THE CATHEDRAL PLAY

The yellow air
hangs in pale sheets
of light beneath
the eyebrowed arches
and talkers stand
in black patches
islanded under their tall curve,
midgets in the house of God.
The actors ended with
their playing now, walk
their last important steps
before the ordinary.
On the squared floor
a clutter of swords
lie sheathed and tasselled
and a shoe has fallen
by a pile of prayer books.
The ceiling spans
mistily above like a
golden dream and slips down
the long ease of pillars
to the waiting stone.
Voices hum round
their narrow listening
circle of ears,
but steps beat
loud upon the ground.
Kings pass us by
unnoticed now,
and Queens with
nyloned legs and
scarf tied hair.
The Author in a

pleasing haze floats past
in half heard
conversation with the Dean.
The Spanish dancer
flys his black cape
in his wake and
after him the last
remaining hurry.
Upon a stone niche
lie the burnt out ends
of candles
the play has with
a final blaze
snuffed out—
and those who lived
it pass into the
dark May night
by the South Door.

TRESCO

Ten to midnight—
gulls scream darkly overhead
tossed on the wet wind,
crying with voices of past Kings
brought here to rest their dead
old bodies, and confine
their slipped souls
in these sea locked lands.

The smooth stones of their graves,
cold Tumulii,
still stand above their dust,
but on the wind
and in the tongues of gulls
they loudly cry
their unquiet death.

Look up—
and search the windy moonless sky
for black gulls sweeping blacker wings.
There are no gulls—
only the once young Kings
seeking their funeral boats
to row them home.

O

in the   window
the mO   On now

fullmO   On e d
is qua   rtered

BLACKPOOL

Alone.
The cold pier iron-pegged
to it's shadow,
the sea-wall's grey stone
at my back,
the sullen sea's brown foam
around my feet,
and the sun
winter thin
not reaching this sad chill
within.

I am alone
no one mocks me—
the pier, the stones,
the sand, the sea,
all of us
     cold
         alone—

IVON HITCHENS

How strange it is
that from the flatness
of this wall
you float me—
float on yellow water
capsuled sun
while our boat
purple hulled
drifts beyond
the glass,
anemones
red as lips
gape.
How strange
to wander
down a brown lane
to the green O
or green water
slip through a brown hole
beyond the frame.
It is hard now—
now I am of your colour
and your coolness
to go out
into the wet street.

THE WALKER

I have soiled with clumsy tread
the virgin snow—
        and led
a trail of muffled marks
        stepping deep
            which creep
                behind me.

Soon white flakes, thick whirling
                    swift swirling
will smooth my steps.
Where I came from
        or how—
      none shall know.
          Nor where I go.

CRASH OF A LIGHTNING JET

What awful tree of tearing curling flame
leapt in the sky to quickly spread black clouds
twisted with fire, the fire no hand could tame,
which burnt with fearful greed, while greying shrouds
of smoke wrapped all the tortured metal round.
What hell, what sudden fierce erupted hell
pillared from this now seared and blackened ground
where as I watched both man and Lightning fell.

So swift this funeral pyre flared in the sky
blossomed the dreadful flower upon his death,
and then as swift again I saw it die
Pilot and Plane extinguished in one breath.

No flowers upon this grave, no carven name
but unforgettable, that final flame.

THE OTTER SKIN RUG

How long ago since night
dropped darkly down
and you, poor empty skin
whistled your mate?
How long ago since light
was seen by those sad holes
of eyes? When life within
was warm not dust.
How long ago since fight
quivered those hollow paws?
When did death win
the awful right
to enter in
that bullet hole?

In your last holt
you did the first great Maker meet,
I stay—
and see each day
the pathos of your little feet.

THE MUNDESLEY FARM

Under my sandalled feet
the tired cliff shoulders
back its earthy load.
Sand grains flown and blown by the gull hung wind
trickle down its rabbit burrowed bosom
in slow count of time.
The summer sky is stretched asleep
above the gently nudging sea,
and sleeping, mirrors all its easy face
upon the water's moving glass.
There at the lacey edge of foam
the naked shore lazes in golden grace
leaning long sandy fingers
up the rocky cracks that
crease the crumbling cliff.
A stone bounds like a
frightened animal down
the steep length and the dry dust
sifts after it.
Here has the greedy sea with tearing hands
with awful strength, torn at the helpless cliff
and in the ragged storm tossed days
and roaring raging nights
mauled at the shrinking edge
pounded the slanting walls
and swept them like the dust before the wind
like chaff, like spray,
into the ceaseless maw of churning tides,
till like the dust,
the chaff, the spray,
they are nothing
nothing—
only a flesh wound

gaping red earthed
on the steep flank,
and the life blood,
the soil, the grains
of sand, run down
the hour glass face.
Here where I stand, the wind licking my legs,
a gravelled path ends,
cut short
walking itself out into air—
and near it tufted with harsh grass
a farm track wobbles deep rutted
to the edge, then breaks in space
like the snapping of a twig.

Once as a child I ran
this yellow length of path,
and in the void where now
the seagulls scream their jokes,
ran to the open farmhouse door
ran on the kitchen flags
buttery cool to my bare feet.
Once as a child I walked
the lazy milky cows along this
uneven track, where now
the salty air blows keen
where solid earth has been,
and with their velvet noses
wet upon my skin
led them past the farm
sunning its windowed self
under a coverlet of roses,
to the wind scoured cliff.
Now is that green dream
as the grey dust

the chaff, the spray,
nothing, swirling
in the wetness,
nothing.

Once in the farmhouse door
with night easing the groaning sea
and the round moon sharp-shadowing
the rambling house,
my first love kissed me—
Now are my tears
salt spray upon the wind
and his lips pressed
to dust.
—and that loved home
slipped like a passing life,
with no complaint,
into the avid sea
that prowls the winter round.

There where it stood,
where the deep roots of family grew
is nothing—
and underneath and undermining still
the sea in hunger waits,
edging the land away,
twitching a slip of sand,
a wind fistful of earth
blown to the air
blown to nothing,
nothing,
nothing—

BUTTERFLIES

Yellow butterflies
one and one
zig
     zag
crazy
in the sun
yellow flutter
butter yellow
falling lifting
two to one
flutter yellow
flat wing
yellow
     zig
zag
     crazy
in the sun.

MOONLIGHT

Moonlight
has spread across
the wet bed of the bay,
is quartered
by the window struts
and falls
in four bright oblongs
on my floor.

Outside
it glitters
on the damp sand,
moves hummocky
upon the sea,
—but here
it lies flat,
flat on the lino,
caught like me
in the shut-door silence
of my room.

SPARROWS

Sparrows
    fight
        falling
            down
in a brown
feathered tangle
four winged
feathered fury
up   up
    down   down
a last
dust squabble
then one
    flys off
        alone
the other preens
pre flight
  lifted
a   wing

TAMARISK TREE

I know an island
where a wind-bent
tamarisk grows
from a cottage hearth,
and spreads over
moss-lain lovers
fine fronds
of feathery green,
then later
filters sharp moonlight
onto their faces
so they remember
—on other nights—
the island
and the shadows
of the tamarisk tree.

THE WREATH

Now in the evening's cool I gather flowers for you,
sweet scented and damp petalled with the early dew
pink clustered roses, cottage bunched on thorny stems
and pale, pale peonies, white faded at their flouncy hems.
A thrush sang in the beech tree as I broke a branch,
and breaking set the whole bough, purple leaved adance.
For you I took the whole bouquet all wedding white
from the syringa bush that its smell would delight—
    delight? delight?
Now that you are not here, I gather flowers for you.

COMINO FORT, 1695

This Fort was built four hundred years ago,
and every sandstone block was cut by hand,
brought to this empty Island in the slow
rowed galley boat, dragged up the sunbaked land
by sullen slaves beaten by sun and whips.
Then slowly foot by foot it towered above
surrounding rocks and sea, so trading ships
no longer risked their goods in every cove.
Death knew the building and defending well
many a harvest has he reaped in blood,
yet now the yellow shade, and distant smell
of wild thyme only tells of peace and good.
—and when four centuries have passed again
will only stones and memories remain?

COMINO

Cicero knew this Island
saw the arrow darting lizards
waiting head up
till the bow of fear
strung them to flight.
Already with the sun
a handspan high
bees are busy
on the cushioned thyme
while larks are overhead.
Somewhere a heavy snail
is birdcracked on a stone.
These things apart
I am alone—
but why did no-one
ever say
that English larks sing here?

KING CHARLES' CASTLE, TRESCO

Through this stone window frame
there always was the sea
moving between the islands,
always the aching white of sand
uncovered at low tide.
Little has changed.
Only that clouds replace the roof,
and all the elements delight
in entering unasked
through doorway, ceiling, walls,
and through this window frame.

ROCKPOOL IN MOONLIGHT

Under the watchful moon the sand is white
pitted with night,
and hunched with pocketed hand
my fluid shadow smooths
the way ahead.
A rockpool brighter than an eye
winks once, then stares,
—and standing still I see
my moon thrown arm
far longer than the truth
reach for the pool
to snuff its light.

LONELIEST OF LANDS

Are there no skylark's high-held songs for you,
no hushing of grass as the wind weaves through,
or rustle of leaves on the lilac tree?

Do you not hear the pollen-bright bee
buzz in the foxglove? I know you can see
the high flying swifts, but what of their scream?

Are there no sounds in the stone riding stream,
no plop with the sudden quick-swirling gleam
of a fly risen fish, no moorhen's harsh cry?

What of the question—why was it I
born with no hearing? Why was it I?
Knowing the while you will hear no reply.

Yet you—born to silence, in love and in tears,
remember your childhood's untellable fears
and help by your eyes, touch and talking of hands
the deaf child's hard path through the loneliest of lands.

WALKING TO BRYHER

Neaptide—eighteen feet of drowning water
fled from this channel, as if the Islands
had stood up and the sea drained from their sands
Tresco and Bryher edging the crater.
With shoes in hand we walk the shell sharp beach
stumbling between wet rocks and flabby weed
which lie at low tide mark, paying great heed
to time, for we must cross that stretch to reach
the other shore, turning before the tide.
Northwards, the Hangman's rock stands sandy based,
by Samson, Puffin rock is seabird faced—
but here the Southward channel's open wide.
In two hours' time our neaptide path will be
hidden for half a year beneath the sea.

FESTA

The sea has become frivolous
slap-happy sunday feeling
ruffled and glinting
snatching foam
from rocks
drumming into hidden holes
flattening footsteps
and throwing white spray
at the cliff face.
It is Festa today,
fireworks,
even in the afternoon
crack black into the sky.
Later dark seas
will sparkle
from the moon
and skies will match
her gaiety with
false bright stars,
red bursts,
and brilliant
night flung rockets.

FOR JAMES KIRKUP

Will you pick your own wreath?
You say the Poet is no more.
What will you lie beneath
forgetmenots or hellebore?
No wait—
let us who fashioned laurel leaves
weave in a circle, paper, pens,
then should you waken there will be
waiting, unwritten poetry.

EPITAPH

We who are left behind—weep
for us the long drawn night
holds in its dark no sleep
for us no peace.

You who have gone from us—sleep
wrapped in the final peace
lying where none may weep
wrapped in all night.

We shall not see you wake—who weep
our eyes are closed
We see your eyes are shut—who sleep
whilst you awake.

CHRISTMAS

Now in this early snow's soft white
think of that blessèd Infant's hands
stretched to light,
and in the hollyberries red
remember the cruel nailing
when they bled.

OLD GRIMSBY

Behind the yellow-hair spiked dunes
where soft sand seeps
in wind smoothed sweeps,
the narrow lane lies quiet.
Forgotten and unused
except by birds and mice,
the brambles snake across
the track to tangle in the air.

I walk there,
hidden from the wind,
deep mark the sands
and pull thorn hands
from off my sleeve.

Most people use the other path
but I
shall always walk
this tangled lane,
this old forgotten way—
it so lonely,
and myself
alone.

HEADLINES ON AFRICA

Ten dead in Riots.

Flies crazy about the kicked head
with no hair, only brains
soft brains and thin blood
puddinged together.

Ten dead in riots.

A crimson map soaks in the dirt
waxen face stares
flies seething for eyes.

Flies survive.

Under bone hands, locked finally over
bowels snaking obscenely ooze wetly out,
flies blackly mass,
feverish, egg-laying, long tongued mass
in the dark wounds.

Ten dead in riots.

Later the eggs will hatch,
flies survive.